*Tecumseh and
the Indian
Confederation*

TECUMSEH AND THE
INDIAN CONFEDERATION

In the decade before the War of 1812, Tecumseh, a chief of the Shawnee tribe, struggled to unite the tribes east of the Mississippi into a strong confederation. He hoped, through the united strength of all Indians, to oppose further American takeover of tribal lands, and establish an Indian nation in the Northwest Territory, an area that included the present states of Ohio, Indiana, Illinois, Michigan, and Wisconsin. The courage and outstanding character of this greatest of all American Indians drew praise and admiration from foe as well as friend. His death on the battlefield forever doomed a union of the American Indians.

PRINCIPALS

TECUMSEH, Shawnee Indian chief who tried to unite all Indians east of the Mississippi into a strong confederation. He hoped to establish an Indian nation in the Northwest Territory.

WILLIAM HENRY HARRISON, governor of the Northwest Territory who sought to pacify the area by turning the Indians into an agrarian society, dependent on the United States government for their everyday needs. He used every weapon at his command to frustrate Tecumseh's dream of an empire.

THE PROPHET, Tecumseh's brother and spiritual leader of the united Indians. He derived his strength from his distinguished brother. Prophecies attributed to the Prophet were actually passed on to him by Tecumseh.

SIR ISAAC BROCK, major-general in the British Army and President of Upper Canada. Noted for his wise leadership and personal bravery, this distinguished officer befriended Tecumseh. His death during the early months of the war was a great loss to the Indians.

THOMAS JEFFERSON, president of the United States. He appointed William Henry Harrison as governor of the Northwest Territory and established the Indian policy that Harrison followed in his relations with the tribes of the Territory.

ANTHONY WAYNE, Revolutionary War hero and general in the United States army. He commanded the American Legion in its great victory at the Battle of Fallen Timbers.

WILLIAM HULL, brigadier-general in the United States army and governor of the Michigan Territory at the beginning of the War of 1812. He surrendered Detroit to a combined British and Indian force early in the war.

HENRY PROCTOR, colonel, later brigadier in the British army. Although allied with Tecumseh, the two men hated each other. He became commander of the British army after Brock's death. His lack of courage helped bring about the downfall of the Confederation.

A FOCUS BOOK

Tecumseh and the Indian Confederation, 1811-1813

The Indian Nations East of the Mississippi Are Defeated

by Joseph B. Icenhower

FRANKLIN WATTS, INC.
NEW YORK / 1975

Cover design by Ginger Giles
Map by Thomas R. Funderburk

Pictures courtesy of: Bettmann Archives: 40; Charles Phelps Cushing: 11; Library of Congress: 5, 7, 16, 19, 22, 28, 32, 45, 49, 58, 63, 70, 74; The Metropolitan Museum of Art, Bequest of Charles Allen Munn, 1924: 8; *The Naval Monument* (Boston: George Clark, 1840): 66–67; New York Public Library Picture Collection: 31; Ohio Department of Development: 27; The Public Archives of Canada: 54; Smithsonian Office of Anthropology, Bureau of American Ethnology Collection: iv.

Library of Congress Cataloging in Publication Data

Icenhower, Joseph Bryan.
    Tecumseh and the Indian confederation 1811–1813.

    (A Focus book)
    SUMMARY: Traces the events leading up to the defeat of Tecumseh's efforts to build a confederated Indian nation in the early 1800's.
    Bibliography: p.
    1. Tecumseh, Shawnee chief, 1768–1813–Juvenile literature. 2. Indians of North America–Northwest, Old–Wars–Juvenile literature. [1. Tecumseh, Shawnee chief, 1768–1813. 2. Indians of North America–Biography] I. Title.
E99.S35I27   970.3 [B] [92]   74–11353
ISBN 0–531–02780–5

Title page illustration: Tecumseh, from a sketch made of him in Vincennes, Indiana, 1808.

Contents

*Tecumseh and
the Indian
Confederation*

CHIPPEWA

LAKE SUPERIOR

MENOMINEE

Ft. Michilimackinac

OTTAWA RIVER

ST. LAWRENCE RIVER

MAINE

SAUK

WINNEBAGO

FOX

MICHIGAN

LAKE MICHIGAN

LAKE HURON

LAKE ST. CLAIR

WYANDOT

LAKE ONTARIO

LAKE CHAMPLAIN

VERMONT

NEW HAMPSHIRE

OTTAWA RIVER

S I O U X

MISSISSIPPI RIVER

MINNESOTA

IOWA

WISCONSIN

ILLINOIS

OTTAWA

Battle of Fallen Timbers

Fort Detroit
Fort Malden
Ft. Miami

LAKE ERIE

OHIO

Fort Niagara (Buffalo)

MINGO

Ft. Sandusky

SENECA

NEW YORK

ALLEGHENY R.

DELAWARE

Oswego

Fort Stanwix

HUDSON RIVER

MASSACHUSETTS

CONNECTICUT

NEW YORK

RHODE ISLAND

I O W A

Fort Madison

Fort Dearborn (Chicago)

K I C K A P O O

ILLINOIS RIVER

TIPPECANOE R.

Prophet's Town

Battle of Tippecanoe

Ft. Wayne

Ft. Recovery

INDIANA

WABASH RIVER

MAUMEE R.

Ft. Defiance

Ft. Meigs

M I A M I

WEA

Ft. Jefferson

WHITE R.

SHAWNEE

Fort Harmar

Fort McIntosh

Fort Pitt (Pittsburgh)

PENNSYLVANIA

SUSQUEHANNA RIVER

Philadelphia

NEW JERSEY

DELAWARE

New York

P E O R I A

MISSOURI RIVER

Ft. Washington (Cincinnati)

MARYLAND

Baltimore

VIRGINIA

O S A G E

St. Louis • Cahokia

Kaskaskia
Fort Massac

Vincennes

Ft. Steuben • Louisville

OHIO RIVER

KENTUCKY

CUMBERLAND RIVER

WEST VIRGINIA

Richmond

JAMES RIVER

Roanoke

ROANOKE RIVER

Norfolk

MISSOURI

ARKANSAS

WHITE RIVER

CUMBERLAND GAP

Nashville • Knoxville •

TENNESSEE

NORTH CAROLINA

PEE DEE RIVER

Raleigh •

ARKANSAS RIVER

C H I C K A S A W

MISSISSIPPI RIVER

TENNESSEE RIVER

C H E R O K E E

ALABAMA

GEORGIA

SOUTH CAROLINA

Fort Strother

Columbia •

LOUISIANA

RED RIVER

C H O C T A W

PEARL RIVER

Fort Confederation

TOMBIGBEE RIVER

ALABAMA RIVER

C R E E K

Fort Mims

CHATTAHOOCHEE RIVER

FLINT RIVER

SAVANNAH RIVER

Charleston •

Savannah •

Natchez •

Mobile •

Pensacola

APPALACHICOLA RIVER

SUWANEE RIVER

ST. JOHNS RIVER

St. Augustine •

New Orleans

FLORIDA

GULF OF MEXICO

ATLANTIC OCEAN

Territory demanded of Western Indians

American-Spanish disputed territory

American-Spanish boundary

Approximate limit of settlement

Proclamation line (1768 and 1775)

Introduction

It started as a deep rumble in the middle of the night of December 16, 1811. Indians as far north as the Huron in Canada, as far west as the powerful Sioux nation, and even in the deep South the Indians of the Creek Confederacy felt the earthquake. As the earth tremors became more violent, settlers in the frontier villages of Kentucky, Ohio, Tennessee, and Indiana watched in horror as their sturdy log cabins were wrenched apart like sticks and collapsed around them. The earth itself cracked open in wide and fathomless fissures as the bone-jarring tremors continued. Whole forests swayed and trees fell in tangled masses. Great rivers changed courses and huge sections of riverbottom farms broke off and were carried away by the current. Lakes appeared where sections of land dropped many feet. The village of New Madrid happened to be at the epicenter of the earthquake. Located some sixty miles below the mouth of the Ohio River on the Mississippi, it completely disappeared.

Wise old medicine men in the far-flung Indian tribes shook their heads in disbelief, but not the young warriors. They snatched their tomahawks and war clubs and headed for the Maumee River in Indiana. Tecumseh, the greatest Indian of them all, had stamped his feet as he promised them weeks before. It was the sign he had predicted that would unite all Indians as brothers. He had even predicted the exact day of the earthquake.

This was powerful medicine indeed. But then Tecumseh was a powerful man.

The Indians'
Situation in 1795

After the American Revolution, the Indians of the eastern United States had been slowly but surely pushed west beyond the Ohio River. As settlers streamed into that lush country called Kentucky, and hordes of people reached Pittsburgh, there to embark with all their possessions on flatboats for the trip south, the Indians lost land by the thousands of square miles.

The Proclamation Line of 1763 was a limit established by the British, beyond which no whites could legally settle or take up land. This line followed generally the crest of the Appalachian Mountains running north and south. The Indians were to stay west of the Line and British officials in the colonies were enjoined to halt westward movement of the whites beyond the crest.

In 1768, the Treaty of Fort Stanwix modified the Line extending it west in a bulge to include Fort Pitt and most of what is now West Virginia. The Iroquois Indian nation of western New York was willing to have the English crown take these lands, which were not actually inhabited by their tribes, in an effort to deflect white settlement away from their country in the North. The Cherokee, secure in their mountain fastness in Tennessee, North Carolina, and Georgia, were also willing to agree to this revision of the Proclamation Line. Neither of these Indian powers lived in, and seldom used, the area involved. For the Shawnee and Delaware, however, the land grant was a great shock. They were the actual inhabitants of the territory and were the two tribes forced beyond the Ohio River. This encroachment led to a stubborn and bloody battle on October 10, 1774, between the outraged Shawnee and the whites at Point Pleasant, where the great Kanawha River enters into the Ohio River. The Indians, led by their chief, Cornstalk, were obliged to retire across the Ohio River after the bitterly-fought all-day battle. Both sides claimed victory, but the whites held the Point.

The Treaty of Camp Charlotte resulted from this battle with the Shawnee. This treaty specified that Kentucky henceforth was white and the Shawnee no longer had claim to it. More importantly, the treaty effectively established the boundary between whites and Indians as the Ohio River. By now the former Indian inhabitants of Virginia, Pennsylvania, and southern New York—the Middle Atlantic States—were all living in an area referred to as the Northwest Territory. It included the present states of Ohio, Indiana, Illinois, Michigan, and Wisconsin.

The dominant tribes of the Northwest Territory were the Mingo, Seneca, and Wyandot in the north of Ohio and Indiana, the Delaware and Shawnee to the south of them, and to the west, Miami, Kickapoo, Potawami, and Chippewa. Like all other treaties with the Indians, the Treaty of Camp Charlotte was sure to be changed, but for the moment there were more immediate problems confronting the whites. The month before the Battle of Point Pleasant, the First Continental Congress met in Philadelphia. It was only after the Americans had won the Revolution that the new nation could turn its wholehearted attention to the Indian problem. Benjamin Franklin had concluded a treaty at the conclusion of this war greatly surpassing anything the former American colonies expected. In November 1782, a provisional peace treaty was signed. Although the Battle of Yorktown had generally ended hostilities in the Colonies, a year before this, Franklin, as the senior American Commissioner in Europe, had delayed and procrastinated in talks with the British. Outwardly, at least, he was being guided by Congress' instruction to keep the French allies informed of progress in the treaty and to utilize their great experience and counsel in these matters of foreign affairs. But Franklin was sufficiently experienced in continental intrigue to play his own game. When most Americans were willing to accept the Ohio River as the western limit of the United States, and British ministers were continuing to insist on the old Proclamation Line, Franklin wanted much more for western expansion. At the same time, his French counselors certainly had no desire to see their former ally become a great nation and threaten their great and good friend, Spain. They would have been content to see the Americans confined to the east of the Appalachians.

This unique collision of world powers led the British to consider it expedient to exhibit generosity to their former colonies and at the same time thwart French and Spanish aims by establishing a buffer state between Spain and England in North America. They also hoped that American acceptance of a generous treaty might drive a wedge between France and the United States.

The provisional treaty signed by the American Commissioners on November 30, 1782, was generous to a fault. It defined the western boundary of the new United States at the Mississippi River and gave the United States all former British lands south of the Great Lakes and west of the Appalachians. Those Indian tribes living in the Northwest Territory now came under the sovereignty of the new nation. And each of these tribes had been actively hostile to the colonies as allies of the British during the war.

Indian outrage at this sellout was immediate. To mollify them British officials in Canada contended that England meant the Ohio River to be the perpetual frontier border and advised the Indians to insist on that line in all talks with the Americans. British second thoughts on their generosity at the peace table led them to search

Benjamin Franklin at the signing of the provisional peace treaty in Paris.

for violations of the treaty by the Americans so that they might repudiate the undesirable features. Finding one—American delay in paying loyalists for confiscated land—they continued to garrison their strong points, now on American soil, at Detroit, Niagara, Oswego, and Mackinac.

Furnished with support from the British, the tribes of the Northwest Territory were able constantly to harass the frontiers of the expanding states. Partly in an effort to protect the white settlers, the government forbade settlement west of the Ohio River and stationed General Josiah Harmar with a few regulars at the mouth of the Muskingum River to enforce the law. In 1788, Harmar concluded a treaty with many of the Northwest Territory tribes that gave much of Ohio to the whites.

The Shawnee and Miami did not attend the conference and continued their attacks on the whites. General George Washington, having just been inaugurated President of the United States, sent two punitive expeditions against the marauding tribes. The first under General Harmar ended in defeat for the whites and the second, under General Arthur St. Clair, was an American disaster.

Emboldened by their success, almost all the tribes in the Northwest took up the hatchet against the Americans. Washington responded by directing the Revolutionary War hero, General Anthony Wayne, to form an American Legion of 5000 men to combat the tribes.

Not until 1795 was the Legion ready for action. Wayne led his men into Indian country and called for a conference of all tribes of the Northwest Territory and the Iroquois nation as well. At the well-attended conference, the Indians demanded that the Ohio River be proclaimed as a boundary line. Wayne could not agree and the two hostile forces prepared for a battle.

As the Legion advanced toward Detroit, Indians gathered their forces at Au Glaize near the British Fort Miami, just south of Detroit.

The two forces met at an area earlier hit by a tornado that had uprooted a two-mile stretch of the forest. Fifteen hundred regulars

*A soldier's wife helps
to defend Fort Niagara.*

of the Legion supported by the same number of mounted militia were attacked by a force of Indians, French volunteers, and ex-Tory partisans from positions among the fallen trees.

Wayne's regulars advanced with bayonets fixed. Their courage and determination broke the Indian defense lines. Once again the first line of defense started an Indian rout that decided the battle in Wayne's favor.

The Indians retreated toward the British Fort Miami, a few miles from the battleground. Wayne had the immense satisfaction of watching the British close the gates of the fort and deny them sanctuary. This one action convinced the Indians that they could no longer depend on the British as allies and that they had best make their peace with the Americans.

General Anthony Wayne formed an American Legion to combat the tribes of the Northwest Territory.

Great Britain's Position in 1795

Very shortly after the treaty was signed concluding the Revolutionary War, Great Britain began to realize that their hasty concessions to the Americans had been a monumental mistake. By granting the new nation sovereignty over the Indians in the Northwest Territory, they had not only alienated their former allies, but had seemingly prevented forever the formation of an Indian buffer state between the United States and Canada. They had placed on their Canadian borders a young, aggressive, and increasingly powerful people that was quickly far exceeding its own population. From 1784 to 1795, the successive English governors, Henry Hamilton, Frederick Haldiman, John Simcoe, and Lord Dorchester, delayed delivery of strongpoints and forts into American hands. They encouraged the Indians to resist every move west and supplied them with arms and ammunition.

British officers and former Tories continued to lead and counsel the Wyandot, Shawnee, Miami, and Delaware, tribes that were actively resisting the American aggressive threat. By 1794, the British had further hardened their resolve by establishing a new fort on United States land along the Maumee River. Above all else, the establishment of the fort, named Fort Miami, convinced the Indians that the British could be believed this time when they promised aid and assistance. Lord Dorchester, Governor-General of Canada,

Canadian governor John Simcoe
introduces his family to his Indian allies.

commenced to build a provincial army around his regular troops and deployed a small navy on the Great Lakes.

Aggravating the threat to the United States in the West were deteriorating Indian–white relations in the South on the Tennessee border. The southern tribes, notably dissident Cherokee who called themselves Chickamauga, started border warfare under white-hating Chief Dragging Canoe. These attacks delighted the Spanish governor at New Orleans who quietly encouraged the raids with presents of arms and ammunition.

Further complicating the frontier situation, President Washington had to cope with an open revolt of his own people in western Pennsylvania, when four of the western counties ousted federal officials in opposition to a Federal Excise Tax on whiskey. This revolt, called the "Whiskey Rebellion," created three years of violence, ending in an armed march on Pittsburgh by the rebels. Washington called out a force of 13,000 troops from three states to put down the rebellion. The army marched west and over the mountains under dreadful weather conditions and finally occupied Pittsburgh without any combat in November of 1794.

During the winter, however, the entire picture changed for the Americans. Increasing concern for the vulnerability of their sea lanes of communication, and fear for the safety of their overseas possessions as a result of France's military successes on the continent, prompted the British ministry to soften its hostile attitude. Then, when Spain concluded a separate treaty with France in July of 1795, her ally England was suddenly left with fewer bases in the Mediterranean. With her supremacy in jeopardy in this vital sea, the British ministry took another long look at its position in North America. Quite soon thereafter, Thomas Pinckney, American Commissioner to Spain, concluded the Treaty of San Lorenzo, removing the threat of Spanish-supported Indian attacks on the southern states. British arrogance and open support of the Indians became an extremely dangerous policy for a nation faced by a formidable array of American continental troops.

But one man refused to accept the inevitable demise of the tribes of the Northwest Territory. His name was Tecumseh and his dream of a great Indian Confederacy was born in the ashes of defeat at Fallen Timbers.

The Shawnee

All but a very few of the whites living on the border accepted the "peace at hand" philosophy after the Battle of Fallen Timbers. There were a few Indian-wise frontiersmen who were skeptical. They knew the young and vigorous chief, Tecumseh, had settled on the banks of Deer Creek, near the modern London, Ohio. Rumors reaching Kentucky indicated he could put in the field several hundred dedicated warriors.

Indian fighters, who had lived through and remembered the early days in Kentucky's frontier-war period, had every reason to keep an eye on any gathering of Shawnee. Throughout fifty years, the tribe had been dominant in resisting white inroads on Indian lands.

Probably no tribe on the American continent had moved as much and as often, or had as many ties with other tribes as the Shawnee. A Delaware legend relates that at one time the Shawnee were a part of the great Algonquian linguistic group, a loose confederation dominated by the Delaware tribe. According to the story, the Shawnee left their homeland in Pennsylvania–Ohio and moved south. Whether or not this legend is true cannot be ascertained, but certainly the tribe was in the South because Tecumseh's father was born in Georgia or South Carolina when the Shawnee lived along the Savannah River. This part of the tribe was known as the Savannahs. They were allied with both the Cherokee, who lived in what is now Georgia, South Carolina, Tennessee, and Alabama, and with the tribes of the Creek Confederacy who lived south of the Cherokee. Strangely enough, however, their dialect more closely resembles the speech of the Sauk, Fox, and Kickapoo, tribes that lived in the present states of Michigan and Wisconsin. They could, therefore, claim a kinship with those Northern Tribes.

The Shawnees were universally respected by all Indians and by those whites who came to know them. They were known as the most competent woodsmen, greatest hunters, fiercest warriors, and among the most intelligent Indians on the American continent. The tribe was divided into five clans, each led by an independent chief, who in turn owed allegiance to the head chief of all the Shawnee. The clans were known as the Maykujay, responsible for food and medicine for the whole tribe; the Peckuwe clan, keepers of law and order and religious matters; the Kispkotha, who trained the warriors in the art of war; and the Thawegila clan, who along with the powerful Chalahgawtha clan, controlled the destiny of the tribe for together they made the political decisions for all the Shawnee. The principal chief was habitually selected from warriors of the last two clans.

By 1763, the Shawnee had moved north to the Cumberland River, then on to the Susquehanna, and from there to Ohio, where they were determined to hold their land. Tecumseh was born after the tribe had settled in Ohio.

The Young Tecumseh

Tecumseh's father was Pucksinwah, a chief of the warrior clan, the Kispkotha. His mother had been a member of the Peckuwe clan. Because his father was a chief, Tecumseh might expect one day to lead the clan, except that among the Shawnee there were no hereditary titles. One earned a prominent position or never attained one. In Tecumseh's case, however, even the events of his birth were prophetic, because on the night of March 9, 1768, a great meteor streaked across the sky from north to south, leaving a fiery trail that could be seen by all inhabitants east of the Mississippi. The meteor appeared exactly at the moment of Tecumseh's birth. To the Indian mind, this was a tremendously noteworthy event and the child was immediately named Tecumseh or "The Panther Passing Across," after a Shawnee legend concerning the panther searching for a home.

Pucksinwah, second-in command of all Shawnee warriors under Chief Cornstalk, was killed at the Battle of Point Pleasant in 1774. Tecumseh's older brother, Chiksika, fought at his father's side and with his dying breath, the chief charged his elder son with his young brother's upbringing. Chiksika was directed to train the boy in every facet of a warrior's role in life and instill in him all the

The young Tecumseh killing a deer.

customs and traditions of the Shawnee. The boy was to be trained in leadership and all the characteristics of his people.

Chiksika took his duties very seriously, and perhaps no warrior in any tribe had a more dedicated tutor or a more thorough training than did Tecumseh. For the development of the boy's character, it was fortunate that he had a sister, ten years older, whose love for her young brother equaled Chiksika's. This girl, known as Tecumapese, taught him to reject cruelty for cruelty's sake, never to lie or cheat his fellow man, and to hold honor above all, for honor among the Shawnee was the paramount virtue of a brave. She was able to instill in him a revulsion for lying and cheating. She taught him compassion for the weak and helpless and provided great depth to the character of her beloved younger brother. The greatness he attained in later life was, to a large extent, the result of this gentle girl's intelligence, patience, and love.

Tecumseh had three younger brothers, triplets, two of whom never distinguished themselves. The third, Tenskwatawa, became known as the Prophet, and was a man with great influence over the superstitious Indians. He was the complete opposite of Tecumseh in character. Crafty, deceitful, and cunning, his only favorable trait was his dedication to the dream of his older brother.

The young Shawnee developed very early and at the age of fifteen, Chiksika took his brother on a raid of a white encampment of thirteen men on the Ohio River near the mouth of the Scioto River. In the ensuing fight, Tecumseh won the admiration of the entire raiding party by his daring and courage. The raiding party hit the group with a savage onslaught from three sides. Although the attack came as a surprise, the white men put up a gallant defense. In the hand-to-hand fighting that resulted, however, they were overwhelmed by the warriors. Tecumseh rushed to the center of the

Tenskwatawa, the Prophet and younger brother of Tecumseh.

camp and was seemingly everywhere at once. He killed four white men and helped Chiksika dispatch another. No other Indian could claim more than two. Rather than show jealousy, the other warriors congratulated him warmly. Even when Tecumseh spoke out against the torture of the white prisoner they had captured, they respected him so much that they joined him in a vow never to burn prisoners at the stake again.

For the next four years, Tecumseh raided with Chiksika, and on each occasion war parties led by these two braves outshone all others in daring and success of their objectives, whether it was just to terrorize a white settlement or to steal horses. To complete the boy's education, Chiksika decided to make a long scout with his brother and twelve selected warriors. The party headed northwest to the land of the Sauk and Fox, where they made winter camp. In the spring, they headed south down the Mississippi to Tennessee and the Cherokee lands. There, the war party allied themselves with the more warlike faction of the Cherokee. Again Tecumseh distinguished himself.

It was on one of these raids that Chiksika was killed, a terrible blow to Tecumseh. He took over the leadership of the remaining Shawnee and raided white settlements with a daring and savagery that made him a legend in his own young lifetime.

In the months that followed, he seemed to be testing his own courage and daring. On one occasion, with only five warriors, he attacked a well-armed group of sixteen white men. Only two of the whites escaped to spread the word among the settlements that a new demon chief led the Cherokee. During this period, woodswise frontiersmen formed raiding parties of their own to track down Tecumseh. Three times his force was surprised by well-armed frontiersmen and each time he fought his way clear without losing a man. One night, thirty white men surrounded his camp as the young chief and eight warriors were just about to go to sleep. Tecumseh heard a slight sound and became suspicious. In a low voice, he gave his warriors their orders, then with a sweep of his hand blanketed the fire with his buffalo robe. In the sudden darkness, the warriors smashed through the circle of frontiersmen at one point. The white men, convinced that their prey had escaped, were suddenly attacked by the howling Indians from the opposite side of the camp and put to rout, with four men dead.

Tecumseh's courage was a positive challenge to every young Cherokee and his fame spread far beyond the borders of that tribe's domain. But as a Shawnee, he realized he must return to his own people in Ohio. He also knew that his devoted followers were anxious to get home.

The war party returned too late to join in the defeat of General Josiah Harmar's army, but Chief Black Hoof, principal chief of the Shawnee, welcomed the distinguished young warrior home with a prominent command just prior to the battle with General Arthur St. Clair's unfortunate army in 1791. The Indians, under the joint command of Miami Chief Little Turtle and Shawnee Chief Blue Jacket, gathered a combined force of some three thousand warriors. Contingents of Wyandot, Delaware, Ottawa, and lesser tribes helped to swell the Indian force. St. Clair could muster only about a third of this number. Utterly routed and driven to panic in spite of their general's almost super-human efforts, this army of militia, built around a few regular troops, suffered approximately 900 killed or wounded in a total force of 1400.

The Indians were elated with this disastrous defeat of the white army. Tecumseh's elation went further than just happiness for his Indians' victory. He saw, as few other Indians saw, that a confederation of the tribes under a strong leader could put together a truly formidable force, one that could challenge any further acquisition of Indian lands.

Fired by their successes against two American armies, the Indians of the Northwest Territory stepped up their raids on the white settlements. In the South, the habitually warlike Chickamauga were

*Tecumseh demonstrates
his famous compassion
for helpless prisoners.*

joined in their raids by the Cherokee, Creek, and Choctaw. These tribes, too, were overjoyed by the Indians' victories over armies in the North, and the Creek signed a treaty with the Spanish governor at New Orleans, promising to wage unceasing war on the whites of Georgia and the rest of the South. These Indian nations went so far as to conduct an invasion of white territory in an effort to capture Nashville, Tennessee. It failed primarily because of inter-tribal arguments.

Tecumseh, in his Ohio home, viewed these cooperative ventures with profound satisfaction. The stage was being set for a grand alliance. As a good friend and confederate of the Miami and Shawnee war chiefs, the young warrior was in a position to both advise and direct Indian actions against the whites.

And yet, Tecumseh, for all his savage attacks, never made war on women and children, and refused to torture prisoners, an accepted Indian practice. On one raid in 1792, when a party under his leadership mutilated a prisoner, he flew into such a rage that the braves responsible for the atrocity ran from him terrified at his anger. Cursing them for cowards, he ostracized the guilty braves forever.

Tecumseh, at this time of his life, was a handsome young man who looked the part of a chief even in the unornamented clothing he wore. Usually this consisted of a simple breech clout, leggings, and an over jacket of the finest and most supple deerskin. Very muscular, he appeared taller than his five feet, nine and one-half inches. He was an extremely affable man and generally a pleasant companion. Many of the Indian maidens vied for his attention and he married one. Her name was Monetohse, a Shawnee girl of the Peckuwe clan. She bore him a son, but became so domineering and such a shrew that for all his good nature, Tecumseh could not put up with her. He sent her away and gave the upbringing of his son to his sister.

For Tecumseh and for all Indians in the Northwest Territory, however, the old life was approaching a climax. The Americans could not let the defeat of two armies go unpunished. General Wayne's Legion was slowly taking shape as a strong fighting force.

The general, impatient at the long delays, had sent messengers to the militia commands in the western states directing them to send their allotted volunteer groups to his headquarters. The whole frontier realized that soon the savages were to be attacked in retaliation for their raids on white settlements.

William Henry Harrison

At General Wayne's side throughout the Battle of Fallen Timbers rode a courageous young lieutenant by the name of William Henry Harrison. Later on, Harrison acted as Wayne's aide when he negotiated a treaty with the twelve major tribes of the Northwest Territory. The Indians had at long last recognized the supremacy of the United States over their lands and their destiny. When the Treaty of Greenville was signed on August 3, 1795, Harrison was present at the formal signing. He did not then realize that the Northwest Territory would be his home for the next eighteen years and his responsibility for almost that long.

William Henry Harrison was a remarkable young man. The son of Benjamin Harrison, a signer of the Declaration of Independence and governor of Virginia, young William enjoyed all the advantages as a member of such a distinguished family. Yet, he cast his lot with the American Legion as a young ensign when that army began to build. He became aide to General Wayne very shortly thereafter and was an extremely competent, loyal, and courageous officer.

After the Battle of Fallen Timbers, his abilities were recognized by the federal government in Washington and he was appointed secretary for the Northwest Territory in 1798. Three years later, at the age of twenty-eight, he was appointed governor of the area by President John Adams.

In this capacity, the young Virginian was given virtually unlimited power over a tremendous expanse of land covering an area now represented by almost five states. Fully aware of his responsibilities and wise beyond his years, Harrison embarked on his governorship with enthusiasm and vigor. He established his home and headquarters at Vincennes, in the heart of Indiana, or Indian country. By the terms of the Treaty of Greenville some six years before, the United States reserved the right to establish administration areas and forts in strategic locations within Indian Territory to the west of the Greenville Line that ran north and south through western Ohio. These areas were defined as six-mile-square tracts and Vincennes, a former French village, was included in one of the zones. It was strategically located for headquarters and the governor hoped to control his Indian wards by his presence in their midst.

Harrison was in many ways a compassionate man, as many strong men are, and made a determined effort to develop a peaceful relationship with the Indian tribes in his territory. His obvious sincerity won him many friends among the Indians, particularly the Delaware. On one occasion, he adopted the son of a dying Delaware chief and raised the boy with his own family.

But the young administrator was also an ambitious man, ambitious for himself and for his country. After 1795, Harrison watched the decadence of the many Indian tribes of the Northwest Territory, and there are many who claim he fostered the disintegration of the tribal solidarity by freely dispensing whiskey at various council meetings and in visits with the Indians. One can wonder just how much decadence whiskey fostered, inasmuch as on the frontier both Indians and whites were heavy and frequent drinkers.

The signing of the Treaty of Greenville by General Anthony Wayne, Little Turtle, and the chiefs of the Indian Confederation.

*The inhabitants of
Vincennes spending a
summer evening together.*

Some of the governor's actions support the claims of his critics that he exceeded his authority, however broad it might be, and cheated the Indian in every devious manner. Stated policy and actual policy were at variance, however, and all blame cannot be put on Harrison.

The official policy of the United States toward the Indians of the Territory was stated by President Jefferson in his second inaugural address on March 4, 1805.

> *The aboriginal inhabitants of these countries I have regarded with the commiseration their history inspires. Endowed with the facilities and rights of men, breathing an ardent love of liberty and independence, and occupying a country which left them no desire but to be undisturbed, the stream of overflowing population from other regions directed itself on these shores; without power to divert it, or habits to contend against it, they have been overwhelmed by the current, or driven before it; nor reduced within limit too narrow for the hunter's states, humanity enjoins us to teach them agricultural and the domestic arts, to encourage them to that industry which alone can enable them to maintain their place in existence, and prepare them in time for that state of society which to bodily comforts adds the improvement of the mind and morals. We have liberally furnished them with the implements of husbandry and household use; we have placed among them instructors in the arts of first necessity, and they are covered with the aegis of the law against aggressors from themselves. . . .*

A far different explanation of the actual administration policy Harrison was expected to pursue was set forth in a "private and personal" letter from Jefferson to the governor on February 27, 1803. It arrived in sufficient time to let Harrison know that regardless of the public policy expressed by the President, the policy was not to be taken too literally; rather the letter set forth a grandiose scheme the President had in mind for the "aboriginal inhabitants," whom he viewed with so much "commiseration." The letter started out with a cautionary statement that the contents were "unofficial and private," but were to be used as a guide in the country's treatment of the Indians in the Territory.

First of all, Harrison was enjoined to gain the love of his Indians by being as liberal as funds would permit. He was expected to preach that the old "free and easy" life for the Indians was fast drawing to a close and that they should take up farming. The United States would supply instructors in farming, weaving, and all the other solid virtues of the white man's existence. Implements and other necessities for this way of life were to be supplied by government trading posts established by Harrison. Prices were to be kept so low that independent traders would be forced out of business. Indebtedness to the trading posts was to be encouraged. In this manner, the Indian as a farmer would realize he no longer needed vast forests for hunting purposes. His debts to the United States' trading posts could then be discharged by selling off large tracts of land he no longer needed. For the necessities needed in an agricultural life, he would always have the government-sponsored trading posts. The directors of these establishments would be glad to provide needed supplies if the Indian could be induced to sign away more land.

Jefferson recognized that Harrison would be unable to gain the "love and affection" of all his wards and in this case he was to demonstrate firmness. Should an individual tribe resent the nation's fatherly but proprietary interest in their welfare and be foolish enough "to take up the hatchet," the governor was to muster a sufficient force of soldiery and drive the ungrateful tribe westward across the Mississippi. This would, of course, serve as an example to all other tribes and insure their domestication.

The entire policy, Jefferson went on to explain, was directed

Thomas Jefferson sought to change the life of the Indians of the Northwest Territory.

[30]

toward the establishment of a series of forts and settlements along the east side of the Mississippi River to counter possible occupation of the Louisiana Territory by a powerful and enterprising foreign nation.

This private letter left little doubt in Harrison's mind as to what the President's plans for national expansion were and what his plans for the Indians were. It gave the governor license to read between the lines of official communications from Washington and act firmly, knowing he had presidential power directly behind him.

It was a good scheme for the settlers, now looking with covetous eyes across the Greenville Line. It also worked. Harrison began a series of council meetings with tribal chiefs under his jurisdiction and after, as his critics claim, liberal dispensing of strong spirits, induced the Indians to part with one tract of land after another. Surprisingly enough, he was able to maintain excellent relations with not only the Delaware chiefs, but with several others as well. There were some, however, who remained actively hostile, although no raiding of white settlements occurred. In these early days of his administration, Harrison saw nothing in this hostility except a reluctance on the part of the more warlike tribes to forego their more or less carefree life.

But north of Vincennes there was a great movement of Indians of all tribes. Hundreds of warriors moved in and out of Tecumseh's headquarters at Tippecanoe near the Maumee River. Many came to listen to his oratory and view with superstitious awe the powerful Shawnee medicine man called the Prophet.

Warriors of all tribes flocked to the Prophet and Tecumseh, standing behind his brother.

The Indian
Confederation

Tecumseh's young brother became chief prophet of the Shawnee
in 1805. This man was, in both appearance and character, the direct
opposite of his courageous older brother. As the Indians from various tribes began to make pilgrimages to Greenville where the Prophet
held forth, Harrison mistakenly believed the Prophet was the head of
an actual movement directed toward fostering trouble between Indians
and whites.

What the governor did not know was that the Prophet was
merely a spokesman for Tecumseh. All the prophecies and the doc-
trine of segregation of Indians and whites were dictated by the
young chief. The movement was but a part of a master plan evolved
by him after the Battle of Fallen Timbers and the resulting Treaty
of Greenville.

Tecumseh had not attended that treaty council and word of
the final draft was brought to him by Chief Blue Jacket, principal
chief of the Shawnee. He had listened respectfully to the great
war-chief, then said with finality, "Someday I will unite all our
brothers and drive the white man from our lands."

Now, ten years later, the carefully nurtured plan was beginning to be more than just a dream. The various warriors gathered
at Greenville no longer said, "I am a Delaware"; or "I am a Wyandot"; or "I am a Shawnee"; but rather, "I am an Indian."

Tecumseh realized that the thousand or more Indians gathered at Greenville at this time did not constitute any great threat to the hordes of settlers pouring into Ohio and the Ohio Valley. He remembered the other Indian confederacies, particularly the one started by Pontiac. This minor Ottawa chief emerged from nowhere to unite tribes as far east as the Seneca in western New York and as far west as the mighty Sioux. But Pontiac's plans were not well laid, nor did he have the leadership and diplomatic qualities so evident in the Shawnee. He did not have, as his successor did, the patience to wait ten years or fifteen years, or twenty if necessary, to perfect his plans.

Evidence of Indian strength in unity was amply apparent in the solidarity of the Iroquois Confederacy in New York state. This tight union of Mohawk, Onondaga, Cayuga, Oneida, and Seneca had for a century maintained the balance of power between former French owners of Canada and the British colonies.

In the deep South, the Creek Confederacy, representing the largest number of unified Indians on the continent, likewise dominated the Southeast. They succeeded in preventing British and Spanish intrusion of their lands for years.

But Tecumseh's plan, even though vastly more comprehensive, would be opposed by an ever-growing and aggressive young nation that determined to expand. And Tecumseh, although aware of the united Indian defeat of General Harmar and an utter rout of General St. Clair's larger army, realized that the various individual characteristics that led to success in these two battles would not stand up against a determined white army. The very strength and courage of each warrior in a wild melee could be his downfall against a disciplined force. The braves were excellent tacticians once the battle was joined but lacked long range strategy. They were difficult to lead and control. Tecumseh believed that by a tireless effort on his part, he could unify the tribes. He was aware of his powers of persuasion at tribal councils and realized that his almost legendary personal bravery appealed strongly to all warriors.

Tecumseh planned to start with the tribes remaining in the East, hoping to draw into the Confederation the whole of the Iroquois nation. In the South he planned to visit the Quapaw, Yazoo, and Natchez, then move east to convince the Choctaw, Chickasaw, Alabama, Creek, and Seminole. As a result of his exploits and popularity among the warlike Cherokee, he expected them to flock to his banner.

In the lake country and Northwest Territory, he expected to unite the Delaware, Wyandot, Mingo, and Huron. West of these tribes, he believed he could count on the nucleus of Pontiac's earlier force of Ottawa, Chippawa, Winnebago, and Kickapoo. The Sauk and Fox he knew, having wintered with them as a boy with his older brother, Chiksika.

West of the Mississippi, he desperately needed the backing and support of the powerful Osage and unified Sioux nation. He visited the Osage and, although they were vastly impressed with his logic and by his oratory, only the younger braves pledged their hatchets. The older chiefs could see no gain for their people in a fight so far from their lands.

With the Sioux he fared better. In council meeting after meeting, he played on the same theme that stopping the white man's encroachment meant freedom forever for the tribes west of the Great River. They listened carefully and respectfully and, by 1804, were convinced this young Shawnee could lead the Indians to victory. They gave their pledge that when the great sign was received, they would take up the hatchet.

In the East, the Iroquois met in council and they, too, were swayed. Not only did they pledge their arms, but promised to keep his plans secret until the sign was given.

After 1802, Tecumseh continually spoke of a sign from the heavens as evidence of Moneta's, the Indians' supreme god, approval for their enterprise. At one of the Iroquois councils, he described what they might expect. When he, Tecumseh, was ready, the very earth would tremble and shake so violently that great forests would tumble. Streams would run uphill and rivers leave their channels. It would be a sign that could not be overlooked and would be so violent it would live forever in the minds of men.

In the meantime, and until all were united, the grand plan must be kept secret. Realizing that agents might report to Governor Harrison at least the outline of his plan, he made every effort to disguise the meaning of the Confederation. In 1803, for example, he had an occasion to calm the fear of Ohio residents and allay any fears they might have of his fostering an "outbreak of hostilities."

A settler, Thomas Herrod, was murdered within sixteen miles of Chillicothe, Ohio. The settlement was in an uproar, fearing heavy raids from Tecumseh's Indians at Greenville. In reply to a request from the village's deputation, Tecumseh visited the whites. He assured them no Indian had murdered Herrod, that he and his people wanted to live in peace and abide by the Treaty of Greenville. The white man had nothing to fear from Tecumseh's people. One eyewitness account of the speech relates, "When Tecumseh rose to speak, as he cast his gaze over the vast multitude, which the interesting occasion had drawn together, he appeared one of the most dignified men I ever beheld."

Meanwhile, the Confederation was growing, and by 1805 Tecumseh had more tribes pledged to him than any other union the Indian had ever known. Strangely enough, the weakest point in the plan resulted from Tecumseh's inability to unite completely the Indians of the Northwest Territory, his own land. It was true that he had a substantial number of followers from the Wyandot, Miami, and Delaware, but he lacked the wholehearted support of many of the principal chiefs of these nations. Among those leaders who preferred to live at peace and hope for a fair deal from the whites were Little Turtle, the aged chief of the Miami; Tarhe, or the Crane, principal chief of the Wyandot; White Loon of the Weas; and most importantly, Black Hoof, senior chief of all the Shawnee. These older men were admittedly losing much of their influence over the younger warriors, but were still a force that provided a stubborn opposition. Tecumseh realized he must have the support of these tribes, particularly his own Shawnee, if he was to enlist wholehearted support of the more distant tribes.

Fortunately, Governor Harrison provided an occasion that dramatically increased the Prophet's standing among all the Indians and aided the cause. Alarmed by a series of assassinations of peaceful Indians by the more militant of the Prophet's followers, the governor convened a council of Delaware chiefs. He scoffed at the notion that the Indian spoke with the Great Spirit, could provide miracles, or prophesy the future. He challenged him openly to provide such a miracle, that if he truly was the voice of the Great Spirit he could ". . . cause the sun to stand still, the moon to alter its course, the rivers to cease to flow, or the dead to rise from their graves."

From some source, probably British, Tecumseh had learned of a coming eclipse of the sun, which would be virtually total in the Greenville area. He told his brother to predict that the sun would blacken in fifty days at high noon. This the Prophet did, calling on the Great Spirit to aid him.

Word of the challenge and prediction spread rapidly from tribe to tribe and the Indians waited expectantly for the fatal day.

And it happened! At exactly high noon on the fiftieth day a total eclipse of the sun took place. At Greenville, the darkness was so complete that fowl roosted for the night and nocturnal animals began to emerge. Although the eclipse lasted but seven minutes, in those seven minutes there remained few doubters among the Indian witnesses of the event. There was just time for the Prophet to call on Moneta to lighten the world again as his followers began to wail and beat their chests. And, of course, at his command the eclipse passed. He had met the white man's challenge.

Pilgrimages of warriors to the great prophet grew larger. Tecumseh's eloquence, once the travelers reached Greenville, won them over. Support came from Blue Jacket, second only to Black Hoof as leader of the Shawnee. Chief Roundhead, an influential Wyandot, threw in with the Shawnee and even the adamant Black Hoof showed, albeit grudgingly, signs of respect for Tecumseh's plan. The rift between the young and the aged chief began to heal. Prospects for the Confederation looked very bright indeed.

In the meantime, Harrison began to realize the potential strength of the Prophet's following. He mistakenly believed the Prophet was the leader. When he sent spies into Greenville, Tecumseh moved his headquarters to a new site, along a branch of the Wabash River called the Tippecanoe. This move came as the result of a generous gesture by the Potowami and Kickapoo tribes who offered the beautiful site to the young chief. Harrison found it difficult to penetrate the secrecy of the movement after this move.

The governor continued to hold council with the friendly Delaware, Wyandot, and Miami chiefs, and in 1809 persuaded them to cede over three million acres of prime land along the Wabash for the paltry sum of $10,550. Tecumseh protested violently, and this led to a series of meetings between the Shawnee chief and the governor. Tecumseh considered such a treaty a violation of the terms and precedents set forth in the Treaty of Greenville. He contended that one or a few tribes could not part with land. Only by common consent of all tribes could such a cessation be made legitimate.

Harrison invited him to council at Vincennes to discuss the subject. Tecumseh showed up with a retinue of three hundred warriors, armed to the teeth. Harrison met this threat by mustering two companies of militia. For a moment, it appeared that war would break out at the council, then Harrison promised to forward Tecumseh's complaints to the Great White Father in Washington and immediate trouble was averted. But Harrison saw for the first time who and what he had to contend with. He wrote to the secretary of war:

The implicit obedience and respect which the followers of Tecumseh give to him is really astonishing, and more than any other circumstances bespeaks him as one of those uncommon geniuses which spring up occasionally to produce revolutions, and overturn the established order of things. If it were not the vicinity

Tecumseh and William Henry Harrison clash over the terms of the treaties with the Indians.

*of the United States he would, perhaps, be the founder of an em-
pire that would rival Mexico or Peru. No difficulties deter him.*

At last Harrison recognized Tecumseh for what he was and
what he stood for. He understood why his commandant at Fort
Knox, Captain George R. Floyd, wrote of Tecumseh when he reported the move to the Vincennes council: "They were headed by
the brother of the Prophet, Tecumseh, who perhaps is one of the
finest looking men I ever saw—about six feet high, straight, with
large, fine features, and all-together a daring, bold-looking fellow."

Tecumseh, on the other hand, recognized in the ramrod straight
governor an antagonist altogether fitting. A clash between these two
strong men seemed inevitable.

British–American
Relations

While relations between the United States and its Indian wards were deteriorating in the West, relations between the United States and Britain were worsening each year.

The Napoleonic Wars were having a devastating effect on the growing business community along the Atlantic seaboard. As a neutral with a large merchant marine, America was in an excellent position to supply all major powers in the European conflict with shipping to spare.

Unfortunately for this intriguing prospect of financial gain, Napoleon issued a series of "Decrees," in effect, a blockade of England. If a blockade was not constantly and effectively maintained, neutral nations, by the recognized laws of the seas, could ignore it. The British navy controlled the seas and the Decrees were a "paper" blockade, since France could not keep her ships off English ports.

The king of England, George III, reacted to this move by promulgating a document called "Orders in Council." This too was a blockade and forbade neutral nations from trading with Napoleon's continent. This blockade, however, was effective because the British navy could enforce it.

The only recourse shipping interests in New England had was to trade with Great Britain and, of course, they were delighted to do so.

President Jefferson, however, was a firm believer in "Free Trade" and countered the moves by Britain and France with an Embargo Act. This Act prevented American shippers from delivering material to either nation. Such an action received very little enthusiasm from New England generally, and none at all from shipping interests in particular. Actually, with British connivance, New England shippers continued to send out ships, heavily-laden with supplies, and in effect became smugglers.

Then the British compounded the breach when *HMS Leopard* intercepted the American frigate, *USS Chesapeake*, off the Port of Norfolk, Virginia. The British captain demanded the return of three alleged deserters from the British navy on board the *Chesapeake*. When the American commander, James Barron, refused, although the ship was on a shakedown cruise, and unprepared for combat, the *Leopard* opened fire. The American was forced to strike and the seamen were forcibly removed from the ship. Public indignation reached a peak, and only the common sense and political strength of President Jefferson kept the nation out of a war she was ill-prepared to fight.

In the Congress of the United States, there was a growing faction, under the leadership of the brilliant Henry Clay, that was determined to pressure the country into a war with Great Britain. Made up primarily of westerners, Congress contended that the new nation would conquer Canada in a few months and that the British could not possibly conquer the tough western army.

When James Madison became president, he found the array of western and southern Congressmen demanding action against the British very formidable indeed. And James Madison was no Jefferson. By the summer of 1811, almost any event on the frontier could have tipped the scales in Congress toward the so-called War Hawk faction. William Henry Harrison provided just such an incident at Tippecanoe.

Tippecanoe

William Henry Harrison had grown more apprehensive of Tecumseh's travels each year. By the fall of 1810, he realized that the
headquarters village of the Shawnee chief had to be destroyed and
the multi-tribe force gathered there dispersed or properly cowed.
Accordingly, he spent the winter finalizing plans for a move on the
Indian stronghold the following summer.

The governor asked for and received regulars from the Secretary of War, William Eustis. The 4th Regiment, U.S. Infantry, sent
by Eustis was not even up to half strength, but they were disciplined soldiers and Harrison believed he could build an army of
militia around the three hundred regulars whose commander was
the battle-wise and extremely capable Colonel John Parke Boyd.

Kentucky sent two hundred cavalry and Harrison drew on
Ohio for another four hundred militia infantry. When the 900 men
headed north along the Wabash on September 26, 1811, they represented a fairly strong army with capable leaders.

Stopping only to build a fort about sixty miles north of Vincennes, which Harrison with characteristic modesty christened Fort

William Henry Harrison
defeats the Indians
led by the Prophet at
the Battle of Tippecanoe.

[44]

Harrison, the army encamped about a mile from Tippecanoe. An Indian delegation visited the governor and requested a council meeting for the following day. Harrison knew that Tecumseh was deep in the South, making a last effort to enlist the Creek and Seminole into his Confederacy. In his absence the Prophet could be expected to meet with the whites and Harrison by this time realized that Tecumseh, rather than the Prophet, made the decisions.

Although the army camped within two miles of the Indian village and no overt activity on the part of the Indians had been observed, Harrison nevertheless was enough of an old campaigner to maintain an alert and extra large night guard.

It was well he did for while the whites were preparing their camp, the Prophet was planning a brilliant victory for his warriors. With Tecumseh away and not able to provide counsel, the Prophet became arrogant and promised the young braves that white bullets would turn to water. Under his protection, no Indian could be killed and the army under Harrison would be wiped out.

About three o'clock in the morning, the Indians launched an attack from all sides of Harrison's encampment. Initially, the braves threw themselves frantically on the regulars' bayonets, their belief in the Prophet high. But as both the regulars and militia held their ground and launched counterattacks, the Indians' fanaticism began to fade. Then as early morning light spread over the battle ground and disclosed how many Indians had died, the remainder flew in panic, with the Prophet leading the rush to safety.

Tecumseh's headquarters and his strong nucleus of dedicated warriors were shattered. Many of the warriors from a dozen tribes returned home, completely disillusioned. Only a few were there to welcome Tecumseh when he rode into a new camp some miles north of the destroyed village, three days after the battle. Trembling with rage, he grabbed his brother by the hair and shook him until the Prophet, screaming in pain, fell to his knees. Tecumseh threatened to kill him, but instead banished him to the wilderness, and tried to pull together his scattered warriors.

Harrison became the hero of the West and Tippecanoe, the cry of the War Hawks. Henry Clay called for punishment of the British in Canada who exhorted the Indians, so he said, to attack the American army. As the western and southern politicians gathered for the Twelfth Congress, they were convinced that America and Great Britain could only settle their difficulties on the battlefield.

The Confederation
and Great Britain

The British in Canada were as ill-prepared for a general conflict as were the Americans. They were certainly aware of the Americans' intentions and Sir Isaac Brock had foreseen the grim possibility that the United States would invade Canada. As a major-general and president of Upper Canada, he determined to build a respectable army of Canadian militia around his battle-wise 41st Regiment and a few Royal Artillery gunners, the only regulars available. Brock could expect no reinforcements from England for Napoleon occupied the government's complete attention.

Upper Canada, more sparsely settled than even Kentucky, could provide fewer than eleven thousand men for the militia and the British general could train and equip but four thousand of these. They were all volunteers, however, and under his leadership could be expected to fight, for Brock was an experienced and courageous officer.

As for Indian allies, Brock was ordered by the ministry not to encourage the Indians of the Northwest Territory in their raids on the American frontier. The general scrupulously obeyed these or-

Sir Isaac Brock, major-general
and president of Upper Canada.

[48]

ders and cautioned his officers to do the same. One exception was Colonel Matthew Elliot, British agent of the Indian Department. His well-known respect for Tecumseh and belief in the chief's ability to bring all the Indian nations into a confederacy led him to supply the Shawnee's followers with a limited number of arms.

Tecumseh spoke to the painfully few followers held together by two loyal chiefs, Black Partridge, a Winnebago, and Coalburner, a Fox, and told them he must now seek an alliance with the British. He realized that much of his work for the past fifteen years had been shattered by Harrison's victory. There were, nonetheless, thousands of pledged warriors who would join him when they received the sign. He directed the loyal braves to return to their people and tell them of his plans to go to Detroit to hold council with the British. He inspired them with confidence that in this manner they would still attain their goal. They were to join him in Detroit when the sign arrived.

Tecumseh had promised the Creek chief, Big Warrior, in his town of Tuckabatchee on the Tallapoosa River, that when he, Tecumseh, returned home he would stamp his foot and shake down every house in the village. This was the great sign he had pledged the Sioux, the Iroquois, and all other tribes and nations for the past ten years. The day was drawing near.

The British were not unaware of Tecumseh's potential strength and when the chief visited Detroit in November of 1811, Elliot, the British superintendent of Indian affairs, held council with him and learned of the status of the Confederation. He did not question Tecumseh's loyalty or ask him to ally with the British. He forwarded the chief's remarks to Sir Isaac Brock.

Even though war seemed imminent, Brock discouraged any attempts to start an Indian war in the Northwest Territory. As late as March 4, 1811, he wrote to Major Taylor, commanding at Amherstburg, urging him to prevent a rupture between the Indians and the United States.

He also told Major Taylor that he was aware of Elliot's deep regard for the Indians but that he should be held in check.

South of the border, however, the Americans spread the rumor that the British were equipping the Indians with guns and ammunition and that the widely separated but stepped-up raids on the frontier were fostered by the British.

Brigadier-General William Hull, governor of the Michigan Territory, sent out spies in early June of 1812, to get information on Tecumseh's movements. They reported that Tecumseh was in daily council with General Brock at Fort Malden opposite Detroit. This alleged fact was duly reported to the government. Actually Brock was nowhere near Fort Malden and at this time had not even met Tecumseh.

It was a different story, however, when war with Great Britain was declared by the United States on June 18, 1812. The British now welcomed the Shawnee chief as an ally and co-equal leader in the coming fight.

The United States
Invades Canada

James Madison, President of the United States, had every reason to believe the reports of increased hostility from the western frontier because Indian raids had increased with alarming intensity, and for a good reason.

On December 16, 1811, the great sign Tecumseh had predicted occurred. Indians from the Seminole lands in Florida to the Huron in Canada and the Sioux in the West experienced the earth-shattering effects of an earthquake that passed all belief. Every house in the Creek village of Tuckabatchee collapsed just as the great chief predicted they would. All over the whole land the roar of falling cliffs, cracking earth, and raging rivers filled the ear. Even the mighty Mississippi turned and flowed north for a while.

The earthquake lasted intermittently for two horror-filled days. Just when the residents were recovering from the first shock, a second hit on January 23, and a third on January 24. Then, as if to show how terrible an earthquake could really be, on February 13, an hour-long terrifying quake caused as much damage as the previous three.

Few Indians remained unconvinced of the great power of the Shawnee chief and hundreds of warriors headed for Detroit and the Confederation under Tecumseh.

Emboldened by these events, the Indian raids increased in both number and savagery and the frightened federal government authorized an army for the invasion of the Northwest Territory. That army consisted of three regiments of Ohio militia and the regular army's 4th Infantry Regiment. As was the custom, the Ohioans elected their officers and, as full colonels of the militia, the regimental commanders outranked regular army's Lt. Colonel James Miller of the 4th Regiment (Regular Infantry), much to his disgust.

The federal government of the United States gave the command of this army to the most incompetent general then in the Territory, or for that matter in the United States. William Hull was apathetic when appointed, but in taking over command at Dayton, Ohio, on June 1, 1812, he delivered a flowery oration to his troops. His promise of an early victory was soon forgotten as the troops sweated to build a road through dense forests and fearful swamps to Detroit.

Hull received word of the Declaration of War against the British on June 26, 1812, while resting in camp near the Maumee River. Along with the news, his scouts brought him word that Tecumseh was behind him with 1500 warriors, that the Wyandot were increasingly hostile, and that some 200 Sioux were about to attack his advance guard. The general, although he remained with the army, chartered the schooner *Cayuga* and loaded his heaviest equipment, some sick soldiers, five women, two boys, and his private papers aboard for the trip to Detroit. The stupidity of this move, since British naval forces controlled Lake Erie and the ship had to pass British Fort Malden to get to Detroit, is beyond comprehension.

The British were understandably grateful when they read Hull's orders and private papers after the *Cayuga* was boarded and captured by British provincial marines. They now had firsthand evidence of the dissension in the American army and of Hull's fears of Indian attacks.

In the meantime, Hull had neglected to inform his far-flung forts at Dearborn and Mackinac, or even the nearer forts Wayne and Detroit, that a state of war existed. With extraordinary caution, he proceeded on to Detroit and, much to the disgust and dismay

*Storming a fort during
the invasion of Canada.*

of his Ohio colonels, failed to cross immediately the Detroit River and secure British Fort Malden, commanding the entrance to that river from Lake Erie.

It took two weeks for Hull to make up his mind to make the crossing and carry the offensive to the British. Even then his extreme caution led him to consolidate his position at Sandwich rather than carry out an attack on Fort Malden, some fifteen miles to the south.

Wary of the savage hordes reported gathering in the surrounding forests, Hull contented himself with sending advance parties east along the south shore of Lake St. Clair and south to the Tarontee River, about half-way to Fort Malden. The northern probe accomplished little more than to outrage the white inhabitants of the area, some of whom were inclined initially toward the Americans.

The southern force encountered British regulars at the Tarontee and after an exchange of fire the British retreated. With a bridge in their possession, the American colonels pressed Hull for an immediate assault against Fort Malden. Hull procrastinated and returned to his headquarters at Detroit to prepare his force more fully.

Tecumseh in the meantime had taken his hard core of warriors to Bois Blanc Island in the river off Fort Malden. When he learned of the American probe on the Tarontee, he crossed that river upstream and got behind the Americans. In a sharp action at Turkey Creek he put about 100 Ohio militia to rout. Hull, believing the Indians were everywhere, withdrew his outlying troops to Sandwich.

Tecumseh, his Indian army growing daily as warriors joined him from the far-flung tribes, took a force across the river and ambushed American parties both north and south of Brownstone along Hull's logistic lifeline to Ohio.

Hull, at his headquarters in Detroit, now began to see Indians everywhere. The British, aided by a force of 450 warriors of the western tribes, captured Fort Mackinac in the Straits between Lake Huron and Lake Michigan. When Lieutenant Porter Hanks, commander of the post, reached Detroit under parole, he reported the circumstances of the surrender to the general. He affirmed that warriors from the Sioux, Ojibway, Menomee, Winnebago, and Ottawa were actively allied with the British and that after taking part in the investment of Fort Mackinac were now headed south to swell Tecumseh's Indian army. Coupled with the ambush of two American forces near Brownstone, this report nearly panicked the general.

The Americans desperately needed supplies en route to the army from Ohio. These were being held at Maumee Rapids by the convoy commander, Captain Henry Brush and his Ranger cavalry. Tecumseh's actions around Brownstone convinced Hull he must send a substantial force to bring up the supplies now threatened by the Indians. Although reluctant to weaken his army at Detroit, he sent a 600 man force under regular army Lt. Colonel James Miller to bring up the supplies.

Once again, Tecumseh with 250 Indians and 200 British and Canadians prepared an ambush of the American force. The Indians fought with remarkable discipline and courage against superior numbers, even after the British force deserted them and retreated across the river to Fort Malden. The battle took place at Monguaga, a Wyandot village just north of Brownstone, and although the Americans repulsed the attack, they were sufficiently apprehensive of further attacks to call off any continued march to the supply train, waiting for relief. Had the Americans known it, they were within a very few miles of Brush's convoy. He had tired of waiting and advanced to the River Raisin just south of Brownstone.

Hull had further cause for alarm when he learned that General Sir Isaac Brock had arrived at Fort Malden with a token support group to take personal command. The American general respected Brock as one of the finest military men on the North American continent. He would have been even more alarmed had he known of the immediate bond that developed between the Indian chief and the British general. Tecumseh and Brock recognized in each other the qualities of leadership and courage each man possessed in abundance. The Indian chief recommended and Brock accepted a plan for carrying the war to the Americans. Although outnumbered by the Americans, the British and their Indian allies moved with determination against Detroit.

Hull, in the meantime, sent two of his regimental commanders, Colonels Duncan MacArthur and Lewis Cass, south to bring up the much needed supplies in Captain Brush's convoy at the River Raisin. By sending with them 350 of his most experienced men, he seriously weakened his force at Detroit.

Tecumseh led a contingent of Indians across the river to occupy the fort's defenders on the land side while Brock brought up artillery. These he emplaced in Sandwich to cover the water side of the fort. When all troops were in place, Brock sent the usual request for surrender to prevent "further effusion of human blood."

Hull, with some dignity, refused to surrender and the battle began. Tecumseh's Indians filled the woods with their warwhoops and chants which sent a chill up many an American spine. As the warriors commenced to burn outlying houses of the village, Brock crossed the river with his regulars and militia. Hull in the meantime had received a report that five thousand warriors from the western tribes had joined Tecumseh, and this report, coupled with accurate artillery fire and Brock's approach, led him to surrender. He surrendered not only Detroit but the force under MacArthur and Cass and the convoy at the River Raisin.

Fortunately for some of the Americans, Captain Brush refused to surrender and returned to Ohio in great haste. MacArthur and Cass were not so fortunate. They obeyed their general's orders, although they cursed him for a coward and worse.

As for Tecumseh, his Confederation began to take shape and his prospects for a truly Indian nation never looked better.

But two men were about to shatter this dream of an Indian empire. The first was Tecumseh's old foe, Harrison, and the second was a remarkably courageous young naval officer named Oliver Hazard Perry.

General William Hull surrenders his sword at Detroit to the British and their Indian allies.

Tecumseh Shows
His Generalship

There was no question that the future of the Confederation looked bright, but Tecumseh realized there were too many Americans west of the mountains. These would not take Hull's defeat without retaliation. Although American hold on the Northwest Territory was tenuous, Ohio, Indiana, and Kentucky seethed with indignation at the general's surrender. Troops were called up and an army under General James Winchester, whose last military service had ended with a captaincy thirty years before, was at Piqua, Ohio, destined to relieve Hull before the Detroit debacle. Placed in supreme command, as the frontier states reacted to Hull's defeat, Winchester's army built rapidly.

William Henry Harrison had been passed over for supreme command because of his youth, but was appointed deputy to Winchester, although, by virtue of his governorship of Indiana, he was a major-general in that state's militia. Kentucky commissioned him a major-general of her state troops and the federal government belatedly appointed him supreme commander of the Northwest army in 1812 with seniority over Winchester. Thus, Tecumseh once again had to face Harrison as an opponent.

For the Indian chief, however, a great loss occurred when General Brock was killed in a battle near Niagara. This left pompous, arrogant, and incompetent Colonel Henry Proctor in command of the British troops in Upper Canada. Proctor, who detested the Indians and Canadian provincials alike, hated Tecumseh, for in the Indian chief he saw all the characteristics of a great soldier which he, himself, lacked. Tecumseh initially made every effort to co-ordinate the British and Indian attacks of American forts and exercised a generalship in spite of Proctor. During the year of 1812, however, he realized he must again make a trip to the South and persuade the great Creek nation and their Seminole kinsmen to open a second front against the Americans in Georgia, Alabama, and Florida.

This time the Shawnee chief was received with unanimous acclaim. His victory over Hull's superior forces electrified the majority of the Creek nation and they pledged their hatchets to the Confederation. Now the United States had two fronts to fight on, and on both the Indians were supplied by British ships whose command of the seas and the Great Lakes was complete. Tecumseh found he had only to go ignite the flame and under their war chief, Weatherford, many of the Creeks entered the war on Great Britain's side.

Back in the Northwest Territory, Proctor, recently commissioned brigadier-general, acting with unusual audacity and allied with an Indian army under Chief Roundhead, totally defeated General Winchester at Frenchtown on the River Raisin. Proctor callously permitted the Indians to massacre a great number of American wounded and prisoners. Harrison, livid with rage, led an advance army of 1000 men to Maumee Rapids and waited the rest of the winter for his army to assemble. He planned his spring campaign, and those plans included the retaking of Detroit and punishment of both the British and their Indian allies for the massacre at the River Raisin.

Had Tecumseh led the Indians at this battle, there would have been no massacre. He demonstrated his compassion for helpless prisoners after taking Detroit from Hull, where only his dynamic leadership kept the Indians from murdering prisoners. The frontiersmen were aware of his character and distinguished bearing. Colonel Wallace of Hull's staff described him as "a tall, straight and noble-looking Indian." William Hatch, also of Hull's staff, called him "one of the finest looking men I ever saw." General Brock probably described him more fully than any other contemporary when he wrote in his report: "A more sagacious man or a more gallant warrior does not, I believe, exist. He was the admiration of every one who conversed with him." He added that under Tecumseh's leadership, "the instant the enemy submitted, his life became sacred."

But Tecumseh no longer had Brock as a co-leader. Between Proctor and Tecumseh an enmity developed that threatened to break up the alliance. Tecumseh had to plead, threaten, and shame Proctor into any kind of action. In one of these battles, the seige of Fort Meigs, although Proctor contributed regulars and militia, the general on the field was Tecumseh.

While Harrison waited at Fort Meigs on the Maumee River for a Kentucky contingent under Brigadier-General Green Clay to join him, Tecumseh planned an early spring assault on the fort. He forced Proctor into supporting him in the operation and led an army of over 2000 Indians and about 1000 regular British troops and militia. The combined forces encircled Fort Meigs and commenced a cannonade. The fort held out in spite of heavy British fire. Harrison expected General Clay and his 1500 men daily. When Clay arrived at the rapids a few miles up river from the fort, Harrison directed him to detach 800 men, as a landing force on the north side of the river, to drive off the British gunners and spike their guns. The remainder of the force was to proceed up the south side of the river. Harrison would sally from the fort to assist Clay in fighting off Tecumseh's

Tecumseh, Shawnee chief
and brilliant general of
the Indian Confederation.

warriors. The American general moved his relief force forward on May 5, 1813.

Colonel William Dudley was given command of the attacking force, aimed at spiking the British guns, and was ordered to immediately recross the river to Fort Meigs with his 800 men, if successful in his mission. Dudley's men carried out their attack on the British artillery with great courage and took the guns, but having spiked them, Dudley left 200 men with the guns and gave orders to his remaining 600 to chase a group of Indians seen in the distance. After pursuing the apparently panic-stricken warriors for about two miles, Dudley suddenly found himself surrounded by Indians on three sides and with British regulars closing in on the remaining side. Tecumseh had seen his chance when General Clay's army split and the Shawnee chief planned a superbly executed trap.

Back at the river British regulars under Captain Dixon charged the 200 man guard and regained the guns. The remainder of the Americans, many of them wounded, crossed the river and gained the safety of Fort Meigs. Of the entire force of 800 men in Dudley's command, 480 were killed and 150 captured. This was a staggering loss to the Americans, coming on the heels of General Winchester's defeat.

For Tecumseh the victory was gratifying, but was marred by another incident that choked him with rage. The 150 prisoners from Dudley's command were put under a small British escort and taken to the ruins of old Fort Miami, a few miles down river. There, with Proctor's apparent approval, or at least consent, contingents of Indians started to massacre the helpless Americans. Tecumseh heard of it and dashed to the area. He felled one warrior with his sword, knocked down another, and called his men cowards. The warriors slunk away in shame and Tecumseh then faced Proctor. First he called the British general a squaw, then told him he was unfit to command. "Go! Put on petticoats!" he spat at the ashen-faced Proctor. Never before had his warriors seen their chief in such a towering rage. The alliance came near breaking at that moment.

The siege of Fort Meigs continued but Proctor received word he could expect no reinforcements from Canada and Tecumseh's Indians fretted under the forced inactivity. Harrison held out and finally Proctor took his redcoats back to Fort Malden.

Two months later, Proctor gave Tecumseh token support on a desultory second siege of Fort Meigs which accomplished nothing. The British general made an assault on Fort Stephenson with his troops and without Tecumseh's support. He was repulsed with heavy loss. With summer coming on, he then returned to Fort Malden in Canada, Tecumseh following him with the greater number of his warriors.

The spring events postponed Harrison's planned assault on Detroit and Canada but the American forces were gathering. Brigadier-General Benjamin Howard with a substantial force patrolled the area west of the Wabash, Colonel Richard Johnson and 800 leather-tough mounted Kentuckians controlled the land just to the east of him, and all the treaty forts and new blockhouses in the Northwest Territory were well manned. The regulars were forming too. Colonel William Anderson and the 24th U.S. Infantry arrived at Fort Stephenson along with the veteran 17th Regiment on their way to join Harrison. The 2nd Regiment of Light Dragoons proudly entered Harrison's camp and the veteran Colonels Duncan MacArthur and Lewis Cass were on their way with new regiments from Kentucky. The picture began to look very good for the Americans, but Harrison knew his future freedom of action, even with his superior force, had a fatal flaw. The British lake fleet under competent and courageous Captain Robert H. Barclay controlled Lake Erie. Operating with this naval shield, Proctor could maintain his logistic lines of support for his troops and Indian allies. He posed

Over: the combined British and American fleets meet at the Battle of Lake Erie.

a greater threat to the Americans by having a fleet that could land his army at any point on Lake Erie's shores.

Harrison, however, was keeping in touch with the young American naval officer Oliver Hazard Perry at Presque Isle (now Erie, Pennsylvania), who was laboring desperately under unbelievable odds to build a fleet that could challenge British supremacy of the lake.

The Battle
of Lake Erie

In a matter of a few hours, the destiny of the Northwest Territory was decided. The American position on the lakes and in the West was completely reversed. The small American fleet under Commodore Oliver Hazard Perry defeated an approximately equal-strength British fleet under battle-seasoned Captain Robert H. Barclay.

The engagement took place off Put-in-Bay in the western end of the lake. Although the ships clashed at a point too far away for General Proctor to observe the action, he could hear the guns. As the hours passed and Barclay did not return, he realized the British fleet had been destroyed.

At this same moment, General Harrison was reading a hastily scribbled message from the American naval commander:

> *Dear Gen'l [Harrison].*
> *We have met the enemy and they are ours; two ships, two brigs, one schooner and one sloop.*
> *Yours with great respect and esteem.*
>
> *O. H. Perry*

Perry's amazing victory gave Harrison a tremendous advantage over the British and Indian army. Tecumseh realized that his dream of a confederated Indian nation had been finally and irrevocably destroyed by a young naval officer who refused to accept defeat. But

Commodore Oliver Hazard Perry
inspects his crew.

even so, the Indian chief assailed Proctor when that officer started hasty preparations for the abandonment of Fort Malden and a retreat to eastern Canada. He became so enraged because the British would not hold on to the fort and fight it out, that he threatened to take his Indians and leave. He was, however, persuaded by the warlike Sioux and Chippewa to continue his support after they received a promise from Proctor that he would stand and offer battle when he had drawn the American army into central Canada.

Collapse of
the Confederation

On September 18, 1813, eight days after the American naval victory, Proctor ordered Detroit abandoned and all British stores burned. He moved all the equipment he could from Fort Malden to Sandwich and concentrated his 800 regulars, along with some 1500 warriors under Tecumseh's leadership, at that village. On September 26, ships of the damage-repaired American fleet stood off the entrance to the Detroit River. Proctor waited no longer. He gave the order to commence a retreat along the southern shore of Lake St. Clair to the mouth of the Thames River. He expected that the few small boats remaining to him would be able to carry stores and ammunition and support him as far as they could navigate up the river.

Harrison, in the meantime, had been gathering his forces for the invasion of Canada. Governor Shelby of Kentucky arrived with 2000 Long Rifles to augment Harrison's army. Colonel Johnson's hard-riding cavalry was in a position to join up at a day's notice. The two former dissident colonels under General Hull, Cass and MacArthur, were now brigadiers and chafing to get at the British. With the army also were some 250 Indians of the Northwest Territory, evidence that all Indians did not have implicit faith in Tecumseh.

On the morning of September 27, Perry ferried the army across the lake to the mouth of the Detroit River. On gaining the beach, the soldiers deployed rapidly but no enemy was in sight. They pushed on to Fort Malden only to find it in smoking ruins. The British had burned all stores, shipyard equipment, and supplies they could not transport.

Harrison detached General MacArthur with 700 men to cross the river and take Detroit. Here, too, they found all military stores burned or otherwise destroyed. The British evacuation of the Detroit River area was complete.

Harrison consolidated his position, scoured the surrounding land unsuccessfully for horses and wagons to replace those he had left behind at the mouth of the Maumee River and did not start pursuit of Proctor until October 2. By that time, he had been able to ferry across the river the horses of Colonel Johnson's hard-bitten mounted Indian fighters.

The Americans did not need to hurry. Proctor's army retreated at a snail's pace primarily because Tecumseh kept demanding they stop and fight. Finally, having almost reached Moraviantown, on the Thames River, Proctor agreed to make his stand. Tecumseh submitted a plan of ambush and the British general accepted it. Essentially, Proctor's regulars would deploy across the single road paralleling the river, supported by their single artillery piece. Tecumseh would support Proctor's men by positioning his men in a swamp to the right of the regulars' line. Placed in echelon parallel to the American frontal attack, however, would be the bulk of the Indians under Tecumseh's brother chief, Oshawahnah. This group would open up with a concentrated flanking fire when the Americans engaged the British and Tecumseh.

As the Shawnee chief looked over the battlefield at the advancing Americans, he knew this would be his last day on earth. The night before, in solemn council meeting with his most trusted chiefs, he told them that he would die in the battle (now known as the Battle of the Thames). No one disputed him. His prophecies had always come true.

Harrison, knowing Tecumseh as a master tactician and veteran

of many ambuscades, deployed his men to expect an attack from the flank. When he learned that the British regulars were thinly positioned in two lines rather than massed for easy shifting to the traditional British defensive square, he held back his infantry and gave the lead to Colonel Johnson's mounted Kentuckians.

Screaming, "Remember the River Raisin!", the Kentuckians galloped toward the British line. Disregarding the whistling rifle balls, they rode in four columns over the first, then the second line. Within minutes the redcoats surrendered and the artillery piece was captured before it had been fired once.

On the British right flank, Tecumseh's Indians held their fire until Colonel Johnson's remaining two columns had almost reached the edge of their marsh. The accurate Indian fire and heavy going forced the Kentuckians to dismount and advance slowly.

Colonel Richard Johnson, however, remained on his horse and led the charge into the marsh. Twice wounded, he still kept his mount until directly before him he saw an Indian, modestly dressed in light buckskin. The Indian fired, wounding Johnson in the arm, but the Colonel's well-aimed pistol smashed into the face of the Indian, killing him instantly.

Suddenly all resistance ceased and the Indians melted into the forest as if by signal. Tecumseh was dead. The greatest Indian chief in American history lay dead upon the battlefield just as he had prophesied. With him died the dream of an empire.

Tecumseh is instantly killed by Colonel Richard Johnson's pistol at the Battle of the Thames.

Epilogue

With Tecumseh dead, the British abandoning their Indian allies with the Treaty of Ghent, and tribes all over the Northwest Territory pledged to the American side, an end seemed assured to Indian–white strife east of the Mississippi and north of the Ohio.

Many of the principals in the Battle of the Thames went on to greater glory. Harrison became President of the United States, as did courageous young Captain Zachary Taylor who beat off repeated attacks to hold Fort Harrison for ten days until a relief party showed up. Colonel Richard Johnson became Martin Van Buren's Vice President. Colonel Lewis Cass lost a bid for the presidency to Zachary Taylor, but held many federal positions.

Commodore Oliver Hazard Perry, probably the greatest hero of the war in the Northwest Territory, died of fever at the age of thirty-four in the West Indies while in command of a naval squadron in those waters.

Proctor was court-martialed, but was treated lightly with only a rebuke for his cowardice. He returned to England and died in 1850.

Tecumseh's prophesies of what the whites would do to the Indians proved true. Slowly but surely the Indian was driven west to ridiculously small reservations. Broken, scattered, and often at odds with each other, the Indians have found no Tecumseh again in over 150 years to unite and lead them.

Bibliography

Barry, James B. *The Battle of Lake Erie* (A Focus Book). New York: Franklin Watts, Inc., 1970.

Eckert, Allan W. *The Frontiersman*. Boston: Little, Brown and Company, 1967.

Havinghurst, Walter. *Land of Promise*. New York: Macmillan Company, 1946.

Josephy, Alvin M., Jr. *The Patriot Chiefs*. New York: Viking Press, 1961.

Klink, Carl F. *Tecumseh—Fact and Fiction in Early Records*. Englewood Cliffs, N.J.: Prentice-Hall, 1961.

Tebbel, John. *The Battle of Fallen Timbers* (A Focus Book). New York: Franklin Watts, Inc., 1972.

Terrell, John Upton. *American Indian Almanac*. New York: World Publishing Co., 1971.

Tucker, Glenn. *Tecumseh: Vision of Glory*. New York: Bobbs-Merrill Co., 1956.

Van Every, Dale. *Disinherited*. New York: William Morrow and Co., 1966.

———. *The Final Challenge*. New York: William Morrow and Co., 1964.

Index

Territory army, 60, 61, 62, 65, 68, 69, 72, 75

as Governor of Northwest Territory, 35, 37, 38, 39, 41, 43, 44, 46, 47, 50, 57, 60

as President, 76

Harrison, Fort (Ind.), 44–46, 76

Hatch, William, 62

Herrod, Thomas, 37

Howard, Brigadier-General Benjamin, 65

Hull, General William, 51, 53, 55, 56, 57, 60, 72, 73

Huron Indians, 1, 36, 52

Huron, Lake, 56

Illinois, 3
    See also Northwest Territory

Indiana, 1, 3, 60
    See also Northwest Territory

Iroquois Indians, 2, 36, 50
    Confederacy of, 35

Jefferson, Thomas, 29, 30, 33, 43
    Second Inaugural Address (1805), 29

Johnson, Colonel Richard, 65, 72, 73, 75, 76

Kanawha River, W.Va., 3

Kentucky, 1, 2, 3, 14, 44, 48, 60, 62

Kickapoo Indians, 3, 15, 36, 39

Kispkotha Indians, 15, 17

Knox, Fort (Ky.), 41

Leopard, H.M.S., 43

Little Turtle (Miami chief), 21, 37

London, Ohio, 14

Louisiana Territory, 33

MacArthur, Colonel Duncan, 57, 65, 72, 73

Mackinac, Mich., 6, 53

Mackinac, Fort, 56

Madison, James, 43, 52

Malden, Fort (Ont.), 51, 53, 55, 56, 65, 71, 72, 73

Maumee River, 1, 10, 33, 53, 62
    mouth of, 73
    rapids of, 56, 61

Maykujay Indians, 15

Mediterranean Sea, 12

Meigs, Fort (Ohio), 62
    siege of, 64, 65

Menomee, Ind., 56

Meteor streak (1768), 17

Mexico, 41

Miami Indians, 3, 6, 10, 21, 23, 37, 39

Miami, Fort (Ohio), 6, 9, 10, 64

Michigan, 3, 15, 51
    See also Northwest Territory

Michigan, Lake, 56

Middle Atlantic states, 3

Miller, Lt. Col. James, 53, 56

War of 1812:
    Battle of Lake Erie, 69–71
    declaration of, 51, 53
    end of, 76
    and Indian confederation, 72–76
    Tecumseh in, 60–68
    and U.S. invasion of Canada, 52–59
    "War Hawks" and, 43, 47
Washington, George, 6, 12
Washington, D.C., 25, 33, 39
Wayne, General Anthony, 6, 9, 23, 25
Wayne, Mich., 53

Wea Indians, 37
Weatherford (Creek chief), 61
West Virginia, 2
Whiskey Rebellion (1794), 12
White Loon (Wea chief), 37
Winchester, General James, 60, 61, 64
Winnebago Indians, 36, 50, 56
Wisconsin, 3, 15
    See also Northwest Territory
Wyandot Indians, 3, 10, 21, 35, 36, 37, 38, 39, 53

Yazoo Indians, 36
Yorktown, Battle of (1781), 3

About the Author

Born in Parkersburg, West Virginia, Rear Admiral Joseph B. Icenhower graduated from the U.S. Naval Academy in 1936. As commanding officer of a submarine during World War II, he was awarded the Silver Star, the Navy Cross, and two Bronze Stars for outstanding bravery. He is the author of several children's books, including *The Panay Incident* (A Focus Book) and *Perry and the Open Door to Japan* (A World Focus Book), both published by Franklin Watts, Inc. Now retired, Admiral Icenhower makes his home in suburban Philadelphia.